D0506912

Extreme

SNOWBOARDING

Blaine Wiseman

Weigl Publishers Inc.

Published by Weigl Publishers Inc.
350 5th Avenue, Suite 3304, PMB 6G
New York, NY 10118-0069

Website: www.weigl.com

All of the Internet URLs given in the book were valid at the time of publication. However, due to the dynamic nature of the Internet, some addresses may have changed, or sites may have ceased to exist since publication. While the author and publisher regret any inconvenience this may cause readers, no responsibility for any such changes can be accepted by either the author or the publisher.

Library of Congress Cataloging-in-Publication Data available upon request.
Fax 1-866-44-WEIGL for the attention of the Publishing Records department.

ISBN 978-1-59036-920-3 (hard cover)
ISBN 978-1-59036-921-0 (soft cover)

Printed in the United States of America
1 2 3 4 5 6 7 8 9 0 12 11 10 09 08

Photo credits:
Weigl acknowledges Getty Images as its primary image supplier for this title.

Every reasonable effort has been made to trace ownership and to obtain permission to reprint copyright material. The publishers would be pleased to have any errors or omissions brought to their attention so that they may be corrected in subsequent printings.

EDITOR: Heather C. Hudak
DESIGN: Terry Paulhus
LAYOUT: Kathryn Livingstone

Extreme SNOWBOARDING

CONTENTS

The X Games are an annual sports tournament that showcases the best athletes in the extreme sports world. Extreme sports are performed at high speeds. Participants must wear special equipment to help protect them from injury. Only athletes who spend years training should take part in these sports. There are many competitions, such as the X Games, that celebrate the skill, dedication, and determination of the athletes, as well as the challenge and difficulty of the sports.

The X Games began as the Extreme Games in 1995. The following year, the name was shortened to X Games. In 1995 and 1996, the games were held in the summer and feature a wide variety of sports. These included skateboarding, inline skating, BMX, street luge, sky surfing, and rock climbing.

The popularity of the X Games made it possible for more sports to be showcased. In 1997, the Winter X Games began. The Winter X Games feature sports such as snowboarding, skiing, and snowmobiling. Today, there are Summer and Winter X Games each year.

Some of the best snowboarders in the world compete in the X Games. These athletes perform extreme moves in front of large crowds. Events feature boarders flying above the ground, performing amazing tricks.

TECHNOLINK

Learn more about the X Games at **expn.go.com**.

X FEST

The X Games are about more than sports. Each year, musical acts from all over the world perform for fans at the X Games. X Fest is the name for the musical portion of the X Games. It features some of the best-known punk rock, hip hop, and alternative music artists of the time. These artists perform between sporting events and keep the crowds entertained and excited for the competitions.

WHAT IS SNOWBOARDING?

Snowboarding has grown to be one of the world's most popular winter sports. This activity is a combination of skiing and surfing. Snowboarders stand on a long board, like a surfboard, and ride it down a snow-covered hill. They can perform a wide variety of stunts on flat ground, in the air, or on rails and ledges. Snowboarders also can race through obstacle courses at high speeds.

Snowboarding first became popular in the 1990s, but it has been around since the 1960s. The first snowboard was built by Sherman Poppen on Christmas Day in 1965. Poppen fastened two skis together, using straps to hold his feet in place. His wife called the invention the "snurfer" because the board "surfed" on snow.

Timeline

1965 – Sherman Poppen builds the first snurfer.

1970 – Dimitrije Milovich begins building snurfers based on surfboard designs.

1975 – Milovich starts the first snowboard manufacturing company, Winterstick.

1977 – Jake Burton Carpenter starts Burton Snowboards.

1981 – The first snowboard competition is held in Leadville, Colorado.

1976 – The world's first outdoor skateparks are built in Port Orange, Florida and Carlsbad, California.

In 1970, a surfer from New York State named Dimitrije Milovich began designing snowboards using surfboard building techniques. He experimented with different materials, such as nylon straps, metal edges, and glass and gravel for the surface of the board. Milovich's company, Winterstick, is considered the first snowboard manufacturer in the world.

Jake Burton Carpenter began building boards with a different design. At first, he called his boards "snurfboards," but he had to change the name because Sherman Poppen owned the name "snurfer." Instead, Burton began calling his boards snowboards. He spent his days trying to improve the design. In 1977, he founded Burton Snowboards. Today, Burton is the world's largest snowboard company.

Jake Burton Carpenter is one of the best-known names in snowboarding.

1986 – Stratton Mountain in Vermont becomes the first ski resort to offer snowboard lessons.

1987–1988 – The first snowboarding World Cup is held. The tournament features two events in Europe and two in America.

1995 – Vail ski resort develops the first snowboard park.

1997 – Snowboarding is showcased at the first Winter X Games in California.

1998 – Snowboarding becomes an official Olympic sport in Nagano, Japan.

ALL THE RIGHT EQUIPMENT

Protection from winter elements is a big part of choosing clothing and equipment for snowboarding. Temperatures can vary greatly from month to month, day to day, and even over a few hours. For this reason, it is important to dress in layers when snowboarding.

Each layer of clothing is suited to different weather conditions and temperatures. For example, if it is snowing and windy, with cool temperatures, a person should wear a heavy winter jacket, warm hat, thick gloves or mittens, and snow pants. However, throughout the day, the weather can change. If the Sun is shining and the temperature rises, snowboarders need lighter clothing so that they do not get too hot. Underneath the jacket, hat, thick gloves, and warm pants, the snowboarder should have a sweatshirt, light gloves, and waterproof pants. Layers allow snowboarders to ride in comfort, no matter what type of weather they encounter.

ACCESSORIZE IT !

The base of a snowboard can become scratched and worn. It is important to apply wax to the base of the board on a regular basis in order to keep it sliding at its best.

Goggles protect a snowboarder's eyes from snow, ice, and other objects that fly into the eyes while traveling at fast speeds. Goggles are tinted to offer protection from sunshine, which can be especially bright when reflecting off snow.

Helmets are essential equipment in snowboarding. A helmet can protect boarders from serious injury if they fall on their head or hit their head against a tree.

Bindings are plastic pieces that can be tightened around the boarder's boots. They can be set at different angles to hold a boarder's feet in the most comfortable position on the board.

The top layer of the snowboard is called the topsheet. It protects the inside layers from the Sun's rays. Inside, there is a layer of fiberglass to make the topsheet stronger. Beneath this is the core, or the thickest part of the board. It is made of wood, foam, or a lightweight material called honeycomb. Another layer of fiberglass below the core adds stability and stiffness to the board. Along the sides of the board, there is a layer of steel that digs into the snow when the board is turned, giving it better grip. The bottom layer of the snowboard is a plastic base called "**P-tex**."

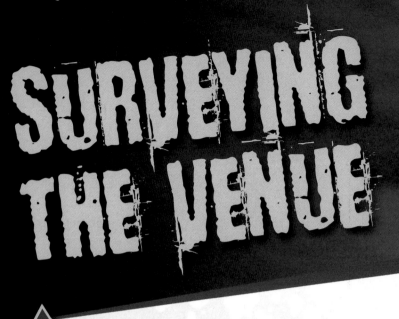

SURVEYING THE VENUE

Anyone with access to a snow-covered hill or mountain can snowboard. Boarders who like to ride fast and race will be attracted to steep slopes and flat **terrain**. Many ski resorts have race courses for snowboarders who want to challenge others to race. These boarders focus on speed and control rather than aerial stunts.

For snowboarders who want to defy **gravity**, most ski resorts offer snowboard parks. These are enclosed areas with many obstacles that can be used to perform **aerial** stunts and tricks.

Many types of obstacles can be found in snowboard parks. **Halfpipes** are a common site at many snowboard parks. These structures have two ramps that face each other and are joined by a flat section. Rails are an obstacle that have long metal rods for grinding or jumping. They can be long or short, straight or curved, flat or rounded, and wide or narrow. Jumps are ramps of snow. Boarders jump off the top, performing tricks before landing. Some of the largest jumps are called tabletops. These huge piles of snow have a ramp leading up each side and a flat section at the top. Tabletops can vary in height. Some are just 10 feet (3 meters), while others are 130 feet (40 m).

For a person who wants to move fast, hard, well-groomed snow is best. Boarders who enjoy performing aerial stunts prefer soft, loose snow, called powder. Powder is much better to land in when falling.

TECHNOLINK

To learn more about the best places to snowboard, visit **http://extremeprosports. com/snowboarding**.

SLOPESTYLE

Slopestyle is an X Games competition that showcases the individual talent and style of each snowboarder. It takes place in a snowboard park that is mapped out like a course. Riders can choose their own route through the course, performing stunts and tricks on the obstacles that they choose. Obstacles include a variety of bumps, jumps, and rails. Both men and women compete in slopestyle at the X Games.

During the 2002 Slopestyle event, Peter Line took to the air off a rail.

Snowboarders are judged on the style, variety, and degree of difficulty of the tricks they perform. Degree of difficulty is based on the amount of skill needed to perform the tricks. Tricks that are considered more difficult receive higher scores. Style points are based on how well the trick is **executed**. To achieve the highest style points, the rider must execute his or her moves smoothly and without error. He or she must have a good takeoff technique, perform the stunt well, and land the trick without falling. Variety is about using as many obstacles in the time allotted and performing different types of tricks. High points are given to athletes who perform grinds, spins, **grabs**, **tweaks**, **handplants**, and other tricks.

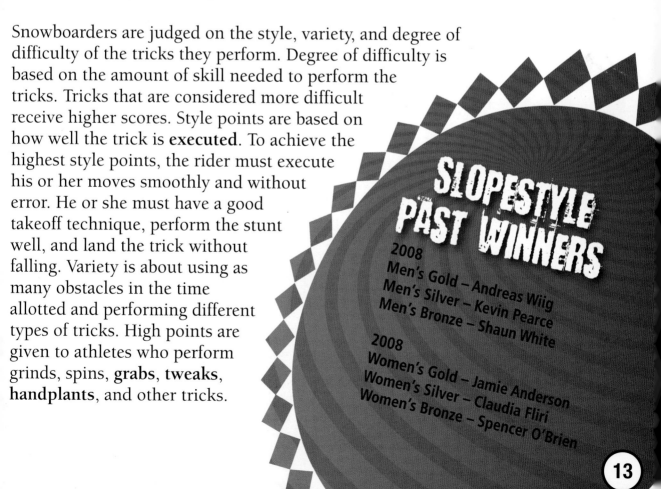

SLOPESTYLE PAST WINNERS

2008
Men's Gold – Andreas Wiig
Men's Silver – Kevin Pearce
Men's Bronze – Shaun White

2008
Women's Gold – Jamie Anderson
Women's Silver – Claudia Fliri
Women's Bronze – Spencer O'Brien

BOARDER X

Boarder X, or Snowboarder X, has been featured at every Winter X Games. It is a timed race event. Six riders compete at the same time, racing through a series of gates, from the top of a course to the bottom. The event is based on speed and control, rather than style and execution. The snowboarder who crosses the finish line first is the winner.

Although it may sound simple, Boarder X is actually very difficult and dangerous. The race course features turns, bumps, and jumps that can cause the riders to lose control as they travel at high speeds. As well, boarders can collide with one another as they try to move into a better position. The course includes a 115-foot (35-m) jump before the finish line.

Boarder X features both men's and women's competitions, and in 2006, it became an Olympic sport.

During Boarder X, riders sometimes have to clear jumps.

BOARDER X PAST WINNERS

2008
Men's Gold – Nate Holland
Men's Silver – Markus Schairer
Men's Bronze – David Speiser

2008
Women's Gold – Lindsey Jacobellis
Women's Silver – Tanja Fredien
Women's Bronze – Sandra Frei

SUPERPIPE

The SuperPipe event takes place in a halfpipe. The halfpipe is about 400 feet (122 m) long and features two 15-foot (4.6-m) high ramps that face each other. There is a flat bottom between the two ramps. The halfpipe is dug out of the ground or a large pile of snow.

Riders start at the top and drop into the halfpipe, **descending** one ramp and launching themselves off the opposite ramp. While in the air, the snowboarder performs an aerial stunt before landing. The rider lands on the same ramp that he or she used as a jump, before continuing back across the flat and up the other ramp. The competitors continue this pattern, until they reach the bottom of the hill, where the halfpipe ends.

Danny Davis practiced his moves before the Superpipe event at X Games 11.

16

Each boarder gets three runs. During this time, he or she can perform as many tricks as possible before reaching the bottom. Participants are judged on style, **amplitude**, variety, and degree of difficulty.

SUPERPIPE PAST WINNERS

2008
Men's Gold – Shaun White
Men's Silver – Ryoh Aono
Men's Bronze – Kevin Pearce

2008
Women's Gold – Gretchen Bleiler
Women's Silver – Torah Bright
Women's Bronze – Kelly Clark

QUALIFYING TO COMPETE

The first step to becoming a professional snowboarder is getting a sponsorship. This means that a company will pay the rider money to represent it. Sponsored riders get free clothing and equipment, and may be sent to tournaments and events around the world.

To get sponsored, a person must be very good at snowboarding. Practice is the most important part of becoming good at any sport, including snowboarding. Most professional snowboarders spend the winter practicing their moves on ski hills and in snowboard parks. They explore different places, including parks and hills all over the world. By doing this, snowboarders find obstacles and conditions that they have never seen before. This forces them to try new moves and improve their riding.

TECHNOLINK

Learn more about how to become a better snowboarder at **www.learn-snowboard.com**.

The next step to getting sponsored is making contact with companies. Most snowboard companies have information for getting sponsored on their websites.

To qualify for the X Games, a snowboarder must compete in certain events throughout the year. The top riders in these competitions qualify for the X Games. The top snowboarders in the overall standings of the International Snowboarding Federation (ISF) also qualify. To rank at the top of these standings, a rider must compete in most ISF competitions. Top performers from the previous year's X Games also qualify.

SIMILAR SPORTS

While snowboarding is a unique sport, it is not the only sport in which the athlete rides on a board or on a snow-covered hill. These sports are similar to snowboarding.

Wakeboarding

Wakeboarding developed from surfing and water skiing. Like snowboarding, the athlete rides a board. However, instead of riding on snow, the rider glides across water holding onto a rope that is attached to a motorboat. The boat tows the wakeboarder through the water at high speeds. The rider uses the wake as a jump and performs aerial stunts behind the boat.

Wakeboarding can be done on almost any smooth body of water where motorboats are allowed. Some of the best places for wakeboarding are California, Costa Rica, Australia, and Greece.

Surfing

Surfing is a sport where the athlete stands on a board and rides a wave of water. It is the model for all other board sports today. People surf in many places around the world. People can surf any place there are powerful, rolling waves. Most people surf in ocean breaks. Some of the most common places for surfing are Hawai'i, California, Australia, and Brazil.

Skateboarding

Skateboarding was developed as a way for surfers to practice their moves when they were not in the water. It has grown to become one of the most popular sports in the world. A skateboard is a wooden board with wheels attached to the bottom. Skaters ride the board over concrete, pavement, wood, and other flat surfaces. They use ramps to propel themselves into the air and perform aerial stunts. Skaters can grind rails and ledges, much like snowboarders can.

Skiing

In skiing, the athlete stands on two long planks, called skis, and travels across snow. A popular form of skiing is alpine, or downhill, skiing. Alpine skiers ride skis down a snow-covered hill. Skiers can do jumps, perform tricks, and race through courses. Skiing originated in Norway as a form of transportation over snow. *Ski* is a Norwegian word meaning "split wood."

UNFORGETTABLE MOMENTS

Throughout the history of the X Games, there have been many unforgettable moments. These include record-breaking wins, long falls, and new tricks.

At the 2002 Winter X Games in Aspen, Colorado, Shaun Palmer, who had won six X Games gold medals, was competing in his final X Games. He was trying to win his seventh gold medal before retiring. In the semi-finals of the Boarder X, Palmer was in first place as he approached the final jump before the finish line. When he hit the jump, Palmer lost control and caught an edge on the landing. He fell straight forward, smashing his face into the ground. The impact of the fall knocked him unconscious, but his race was not over. Palmer was going so fast when he fell that he slid over the finish line, face down in the snow, still unconscious. Amazingly, Palmer was not seriously injured. He won the race, but was unable to compete in the final.

In 2004, at only 17 years old, Hannah Teter won the SuperPipe gold medal at the Winter X Games in Aspen. It was her first X Games gold medal. Teter had already won the competition, and she decided to finish the X Games in style. For her final run, Teter took off her jacket and rode the halfpipe wearing a tank top. With her bare arms exposed to the cold and snow, Teter fell hard as she tried to land a trick. Falling and sliding face-first down the halfpipe wall, Teter's helmet came off, but she continued to plow through the snow. Although she was not injured, when she stopped sliding and stood up, Teter's face and arms were covered in snow. The fall could have been painful and embarrassing, but Teter laughed about it. Before accepting her gold medal, she said "Ooh, that's cold!"

In 2006, at Winter X Games 10, 19-year-old Shaun White won his fourth straight X Games Slopestyle gold medal. White won the gold with a flawless run that included three 1080s, or three full 360° rotations in the air, and one 900, two and a half 360° rotations in the air. In addition, White won his second SuperPipe gold medal this same year.

AROUND THE WORLD

Lake Louise, Canada

Lake Louise is one of the largest ski and snowboard areas in North America, with 4,200 acres (1,700 hectares) of terrain. At Lake Louise, there are runs suitable for all skill levels. There also is a snowboard park that offers a variety of rails, jumps, and some of the best snow in the world.

ATLANTIC OCEAN

Heavenly, United States

Located on the shore of Lake Tahoe, Heavenly is the largest ski and snowboard resort in California. Heavenly has 4,800 acres (1,942 hectares) of terrain and 95 trails. There are two snowboard parks and nine halfpipes.

PACIFIC OCEAN

Jackson Hole, United States

Located in the Teton range of the Rocky Mountains in Wyoming, Jackson Hole offers two mountains—Rendezvous and Apres Vous. Adding up to 2,500 acres (1,012 hectares) of terrain, Jackson Hole has runs appropriate for every skill level. There are well-groomed slopes for beginners, and a snowboard park and Superpipe for more skilled snowboarders.

X Games Venues

1. Aspen, United States
2. Big Bear Lake, United States
3. Crested Butte, United States
4. Mount Snow, United States
5. Whistler Blackcomb, Canada

ARCTIC OCEAN

ARCTIC OCEAN

Chamonix, France

Located in the French Alps, Chamonix is a great resort for families, as well as single riders and small groups. Open from December until May, Chamonix offers three main areas for snowboarders with advanced skills or a sense of adventure, and three smaller areas for beginners. With 145 trails and terrain covering 30,000 acres (12,141 hectares), Chamonix has plenty of adventure for snowboarders of all skill levels.

Falls Creek, Australia

Falls Creek is one of Australia's largest ski and snowboard resorts. The Australian snowboard season runs from June until October. Falls Creek offers four snowboard parks and more than 90 runs for all skill levels. The snowboard parks are rated according to skill level, so boarders can choose where they want to ride.

PACIFIC OCEAN

Portillo, Chile

Portillo, located in the Andes Mountains, is the oldest ski and snowboard resort in South America. Portillo has suitable runs for all skill levels. With groomed runs for beginners and experts, the real attraction of Portillo is its long, uncrowded slopes and deep powder. It also maintains a snowboard park for riders who like to practice jumps and tricks.

CURRENT STARS

SHAUN WHITE

HOMETOWN
Carlsbad, California,
United States

BORN
September 3, 1986

NOTES
First athlete to compete
in both the Summer and
Winter X Games in two
different sports, skateboarding
and snowboarding. Won X
Games gold medals in
both skateboarding
and snowboarding

Won the gold medal
in halfpipe at the
2006 Winter
Olympics in
Turin, Italy

Nicknames include
"Future Boy"
and "The
Flying Tomato"

HANNAH TETER

HOMETOWN
Belmont, Vermont,
United States

BORN
January 27, 1987

NOTES
Won the 2006 Olympic
gold medal in halfpipe

2004 X Games SuperPipe
champion

The first woman to land a 900
in competition

DANNY KASS

HOMETOWN
Greenwich, Connecticut,
United States

BORN
September 21, 1982

NOTES
Won the SuperPipe gold
medal at the 2001 X Games

Won the silver medal in halfpipe at
the 2002 and 2006 Winter Olympics

Started his own snowboard glove
company, called Grenade Gloves

JANNA MEYEN

HOMETOWN
Torrance, California,
United States

BORN
February 12, 1977

NOTES
Appears as a character in the
snowboarding video games
Amped and *Amped 2*

Began snowboarding in 1989
and won the U.S. Open only three
years later

Won four straight X Games gold
medals in Slopestyle, from 2003
to 2006

Was the first X Games athlete to
win four straight gold medals

LEGENDS

CRAIG KELLY

HOMETOWN
Mount Vernon, Washington, United States

BORN
April 1, 1966

NOTES
Four-time world champion and three-time U.S. champion

Often considered the greatest snowboarder of all time

Was killed in an avalanche in Canada while guiding tourists in 2003

TERJE HAAKONSEN

HOMETOWN
Amot, Oslofjord, Norway

BORN
October 11, 1974

NOTES
Won three U.S. Open Championships, five European Championships, and three World Championships

Holds the record for the highest air, 32 feet (9.8 m)

Started "The Arctic Challenge," a professional snowboarding competition held every year in Norway

AUN PALMER

HOMETOWN
San Diego, California,
United States

BORN
November 14, 1968

NOTES
Owns Palmer
Snowboards

Won a total of six X Games gold medals in four different sports—snowboarding, skiing, mountain biking, and wakeboarding

Was named the "World's Greatest Athlete" by *USA Today*

PETER LINE

HOMETOWN
Seattle, Washington,
United States

BORN
August 4, 1974

NOTES
Won six Winter
X Games medals

Has been part owner of several snowboard-related companies, including Forum Snowboards, Foursquare Outerwear, Geenyus Snowboards, and Electric Eyewear

Designs equipment for Burton Snowboards

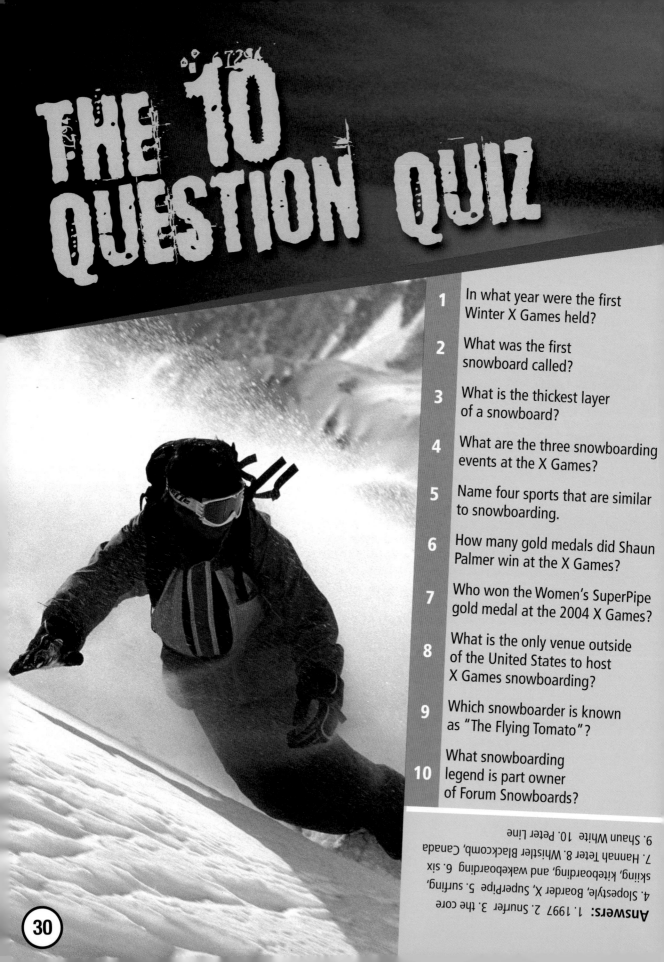

THE 10 QUESTION QUIZ

1 In what year were the first Winter X Games held?

2 What was the first snowboard called?

3 What is the thickest layer of a snowboard?

4 What are the three snowboarding events at the X Games?

5 Name four sports that are similar to snowboarding.

6 How many gold medals did Shaun Palmer win at the X Games?

7 Who won the Women's SuperPipe gold medal at the 2004 X Games?

8 What is the only venue outside of the United States to host X Games snowboarding?

9 Which snowboarder is known as "The Flying Tomato"?

10 What snowboarding legend is part owner of Forum Snowboards?

Answers: 1. 1997 2. Snurfer 3. the core 4. Slopestyle, Boarder X, SuperPipe 5. surfing, skiing, kiteboarding, and wakeboarding 6. six 7. Hannah Teter 8. Whistler Blackcomb, Canada 9. Shaun White 10. Peter Line

RESEARCH

www.expn.go.com

www.abc-of-snowboarding.com

www.transworldsnowboarding.com

www.snowboarding.com

Many books and websites provide information on snowboarding. To learn more, borrow books from the library, or surf the Internet.

Most libraries have computers that connect to a database for researching information. If you input a keyword, you will be provided with a list of books in the library that contain information on that topic. Non-fiction books are arranged numerically, using their call number. Fiction books are organized alphabetically by the author's last name.

GLOSSARY INDEX

aerial: taking place in the air

amplitude: to be very large

descending: moving or falling downward

executed: carried out an action and the quality of that action

grabs: tricks done while holding the edge of the board with one or both hands

gravity: the force that attracts an object toward the center of Earth

halfpipes: two ramps that curve inward and are facing each other with an area of flat ground between them

handplants: tricks done when the rider places his or her hands on the ground or an object and turns halfway around

P-tex: a special type of slippery plastic that allows the snowboard to slide on the snow

terrain: a piece of land and its natural features

tweaks: emphasizes style